PEGASUS ENCYCLOPEDIA LIBRARY

Sports

OLYMPICS
OLYMPICS AND PARALYMPICS

Edited by: Manpreet K. Aden, Tapasi De
Managing editor: Tapasi De
Designed by: Vijesh Chahal, Anil Kumar, Rohit Kumar
Illustrated by: Suman S. Roy
Colouring done by: Vinay Kumar, Sonu, Kiran Kumari & Pradeep Kumar

CONTENTS

Beginning of Olympics 3

Olympia 6

Events at the ancient Olympic Games 9

Participants and spectators of ancient Olympics 12

Closure of ancient Olympics 14

Revival of the Olympic Games 15

The spirit of Olympics 16

London Olympics, 2012 23

Olympics Hall of Fame 28

Test Your Memory 31

Index 32

Beginning of Olympics

History is witness to the fact that ancient Greeks loved sport and most cities in ancient Greece had public gymnasiums where people gathered to train themselves and relax. The Greeks believed that a healthy body was very important. Practicing sport everyday was a regular matter for the Greek men and young boys. Keeping fit and having a healthy body was something that they all enjoyed. The Greeks had four national sports festivals in which athletes from different city states competed against one another. The most important of the sports contests was the Olympic Games.

The Olympic Games that you see today began over 2,700 years ago in Olympia, in southwest Greece. The Games were part of a religious festival. It is thought to have begun in 776 BC. The Games were held in honour of Zeus, King of the Gods and were organised every four years at Olympia, a valley near a city called Elis. People from all over the Greek world came to watch and take part.

As long as they met the entrance criteria, athletes from any country or city-state were allowed to participate. The Games were always held at Olympia rather than changing locations as it happens with the modern Olympics.

Once, all the participants had arrived in Elis for the Olympic Games, they spent a month practicing and training together in a big *palaestra* (a public place for exercise in wrestling and athletics in ancient Greece) or gym. They were only given fresh cheese and water for their meals. All the participants had to follow strict rules. Judges along with all men watched the participants getting trained. Only the best ones were picked out to actually run in the races.

The ancient Olympic Games in Greece began with religious sacrifices and choirs singing. Young men from all city-states were sent to sing in the choir competitions. Most of the spectators were men. Married women were not allowed to watch the Olympic Games at all.

Before the contests the tracks were laid out along the north bank of the river Ruphia behind the temple of Hera and the sanctuary of Zeus. At the temple of Hera, they had an eternal flame lighted, a fire that was never allowed to go out (like the Olympic torch today).

The order of events is not clearly known, but the first day of the festival was devoted to animal sacrifices. The second day began with footraces. For this event the spectators gathered in the *stadion*, an oblong area enclosed by sloping banks of earth. On other days, wrestling, boxing and

OLYMPICS

the *pancratium*, (a combination of the two) were held. Boxing became more and more brutal. Horse racing took place in which each participant owned his horse; this was limited to the wealthy and it was not a very popular sport for the spectators. After the horse racing came the pentathlon, a series of five events— sprinting, (long) jumping, javelin hurling, discus throwing and wrestling. The discus was a plate of bronze, probably lens shaped. The jumping event was judged for the distance covered, not for height. The closing event was a race run in armour. The victors were rewarded with crowns of wild olive, were celebrated by poets and often lived for the rest of their lives at public expense!

Map of ancient Greece

Mythology regarding the beginning of Olympics

There are quite a few mythological stories regarding the beginning of Olympic Games.

According to one version, it was Olympia where Zeus struggled with his father Cronus, finally defeating him and seizing the throne. As a memory of his victory, Zeus started the games.

Another myth tells us about King Oenomaus of Pisa, whose daughter Hippodameia had reached the age of marriage. The king was very worried. He was especially worried because an oracle had told him that he would die in the hands of his son-in-law! So he conceived a wicked plan that would prevent Hippodameia from getting married ever. He made an announcement that any suitor of Hippodameia, would have to compete with him in a chariot race. If the suitor won, he would get Hippodameias' hand, but if he lost, he would have to die. Soon, the chariot races begun. Despite the risk of losing their life, many suitors challenged the king, not knowing that the evil king Ares had invincible horses.

Astonishing fact

The ancient Greek Olympians had to participate nude! It is believed that this started at the games in 720 BC, and probably it was most likely introduced by the Spartans or Megarian Orsippus.

After Oenomaus had defeated and killed, 33 suitors, Pelops arrived. As soon as she saw him, Hippodameia fell desperately in love with Pelops. She conspired with the king's charioteer Myrtilos to help Pelops. Myrtilos sabotaged the king's chariot by pulling out the bolt that held one of the wheels in its place. After the race had started the chariot fell apart at the very first turn. The king was caught in his horse's reins and was dragged to death. Pelops and Hippodameia married. It is believed that the games were held in order to remember the day Pelops won over the sly king.

King Oenomaus of Pisa

Temple of Hera

Olympia

Olympia is the ancient site of the Olympic Games, which happened in Greece every four years. It is situated in a valley in Elis, in the western Peloponesse, Greece. Olympia was not a town, but only a sanctuary with buildings associated with games and the worship of the Gods. Olympia was a national shrine of the Greeks and so it contained many treasures of Greek art. It had temples, monuments, altars, theaters, statues and offerings of brass and marble. The *Altis*, or the sacred precinct, was an enclosed level area of about 200m long and 177m broad. This was the chief centre of religious worship.

The most remarkable feature in Olympia was the Temple of Zeus, the King of the Gods. In this temple was a statue of Zeus made of ivory and gold, a unique piece of art of the Athenian sculptor, Phidias. Next to the Temple of Zeus ranked the *Heraeum*, dedicated to Hera, his wife. In this temple, probably was the table on which the garlands prepared for the victors in the games were placed. Outside the Altis were the Stadium and the arena, where the contests took place. The Palaestra (wrestling school) and the Gymnasium, where all competitors got trained for at least one month, also stood there.

Olympia

Site of Olympia

Though it is believed that the first Olympic Games were held in 776BC, but they might actually have started way long before. The games were held as a testimony to the peace treaty between Sparta and Elis, and it was soon decided that all Greek states could take part in them as long as they respected the sacred truce that must be held during the games. This period of peace was for a month at first. But because so many states took part and people from all over came to watch the Games, it was extended to three months, always during summer.

The sacred truce created many good relations between the kings and leaders. Due to the sacred truce, the kings and leaders from all over Greece had a chance to meet without arms like friends. Olympia became an important place for political discussions and trade. It also enhanced the feeling of unity amongst the Greeks as they followed a single religion and spoke the same language. Olympia was renovated many times, and new buildings were added through the ages. Well-known people came here to watch the games taking place such as Plato and Aristotle.

The 1948 Olympic Games were the first Olympics to be held after the death of Baron Pierre de Coubertin, the founder of the International Olympic Committee, and is considered to be the father of the modern Olympic Games.

OLYMPICS

Statue of Zeus at Olympia

The Statue of Zeus at Olympia was considered to be one of the Seven Wonders of the Ancient World. It truly is wondrous! The Statue of Zeus at Olympia was made by the Greek sculptor Phidias. The building was designed in 450 B.C. by the architect Libon. The temple was as tall as a modern four-storey building, and the statue filled most of it. Zeus's head nearly touched the ceiling. Even in the sitting position, the statue was 40ft high!

It was made of gold plated brass and ivory. The throne on which Zeus sat was made of cedarwood. It was enamelled with ebony, ivory, gold and jewels. Zeus held in his left hand a shining scepter on top of which an eagle perched. In his left hand rested a statue of Nike, the Goddess of Victory. The temple and the statue had survived earthquakes and other natural disasters until it was uprooted and carted off to Constantinople, in A.D. 394. It was lost in an accidental fire in 462.

Astonishing fact

Black athletes didn't win the marathon in the Olympic Games until 1960. Abebe Bikila of Ethiopia did it in 1960 and he did it barefoot!

Events at the ancient Olympic Games

In the ancient times, the Olympic Games lasted only for a day. But it eventually grew to five days. The Olympic Games originally contained one event, the stadion (or 'stade'). It is a race, a short sprint measuring between 180 and 240 metres or the length of the stadium.

First day

On the first day in the morning, athletic competitors and their trainers went to the *vouleutirion*, or council building in Olympia. Judges in purple robes were followed by referees, heralds, athletes and their trainers. Purification rites and sacrifices were made to the Greek Gods at the Altis a sacred olive-grove. The men would make offerings to the Gods like Zeus, Hermes, Apollo or Hercules and pray for their victory.

Spectators who came to watch the events included soldiers, artists, philosophers, princes, and historians, as well as fishermen and farmers. Many would spend time in sightseeing at the temples of Hera and Zeus. In the ancient Olympics competitions on the first day were running, wrestling and boxing for boys. The games were a source of good business for the peddlers and entertainers who would join and become part of the Olympic audience.

> The oldest woman to have ever competed in the Olympic Games was equestrian Hilda L. Johnstone who was 70 years old. She took part in the Dressage Event at the 1972 Munich Games.

Second day

The events of the second day began with a procession of horses, riders and chariots into the *hippodrome*, or horse racing arena. The second day was the day which was dedicated to chariot races and horse races. The chariot races were one of the most exciting and dangerous events of the games. There were both four-horse chariot and two-horse chariot races with distances ranging from 2, 5 miles up to 8 miles.

Javelin throwing

OLYMPICS

As afternoon came, the visitors would leave the Hippodrome and would assemble in the stadium to watch the athletes compete in the pentathlon (a contest featuring five different events).

Discus throwing

Competitions of discus throw, long jump, javelin throw, stade race, and upright wrestling took place. The first athlete to win three events was crowned the victor. The pentathletes were considered to the favourite of the spectators for their overall athletic ability. The second day ended with feasts and celebrations.

Third day

After the second night of feasting and celebration, the third day of the ancient Olympics began with the sacrifice to Zeus. The *Hellanodikai* who served as judges of the Olympic Games arrived and the procession began going around the Altis passing the Temples of Hera and Rhea, the tomb the hero Pelops, and the treasure houses of Greek states around the Mediterranean. The procession concluded

> **The first ever Winter Olympic Games were held in Chamonix, France in 1924.**

at the Temple of Zeus, where priests sacrificed animals.

The rest of the day was devoted to the boys' events who were over seventeen but under twenty. The events that took place were similar to those for older athletes. It consisted of the stade race, wrestling, boxing, and something called *pankration*, a combination of boxing and wrestling. In the afternoon runners ran a long race called the *dolichos*. In the evening, a great, lavish banquet was held where athletes brought their families and other guests. They feasted on meat and enjoyed the plentiful spread.

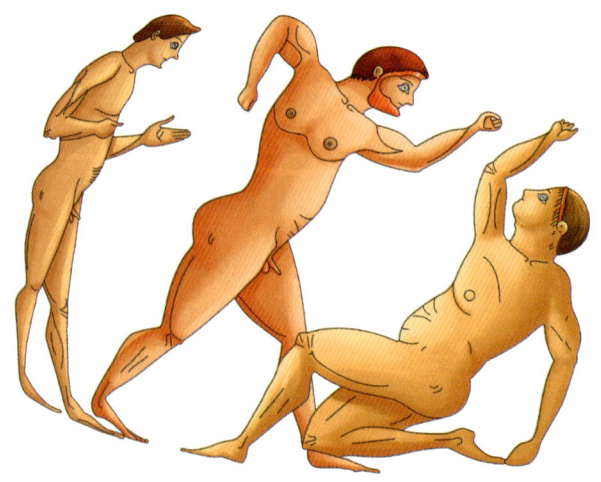
Pankration

> **The first Olympics covered by the U.S. television was the 1960 Summer Games in Rome by CBS.**

Events at the ancient Olympic Games

Hoplitodromos

Fourth day

The fourth day of the competition mainly featured 'contact sports'. The first sport of the day was wrestling. There were no rounds and wrestlers employed a variety of holds, lifts and other movements to make their opponents fall. Three falls and the man falling was declared the loser. In the afternoon, the boxing matches began. Many a time boxers were severely hurt, cut and disfigured and in extreme cases even killed.

The final event of the day was the *pagration*, meaning 'all-strength' in Greek. This sport combined boxing and wrestling. The goal for the athletes was to make his opponent give up and yield defeat. The last event of the fourth day was the *hoplitodromos* or the race in armour. The race served as a reminder that one purpose of athletics was to prepare men to fight in battles. Competitors ran around the stadium twice carrying shields and wearing helmets.

Fifth day

The fifth day was the final day of the ancient Olympics. This day was spent to celebrate the achievements of the victors. No athletic events took place on this day. The ceremonies were held at the Temple of Zeus. The statue of Zeus was crowned with a golden wreath to symbolize his triumph over the Gods. The winners held palm branches in their right hands, granted by the judges when their victories were first declared. In the ceremony, they would exchange those branches for a crown of wild olive branches. Outside the temple, spectators waited to shower the winners with fragrant flowers and leaves. Soon after this, the winners would travel back to their own cities as heroes.

It is interesting to note that if an athlete was caught cheating, he was forced to pay for a statue of Zeus where his and his family's name would be put and what he had done. Then the statue was put near the entrance of the stadium, so that the athletes would see it before the games started as a reminder of what could happen.

Three continents – Africa, South America, and Antarctica have never hosted an Olympics.

Participants and spectators of ancient Olympics

Participating in the ancient Olympics was not a complicated affair. As long as anyone fulfilled the criterias of entrance, athletes from any country or city-state were allowed to participate. But one of the prime conditions was that the participants were required to speak Greek. Participation was limited to male athletes only. Women were allowed to take part only in the events involving horses. In 396 BC and again in 392 BC, the Spartan Princess Cynisca won her the four-horse race. It is believed that single women (not betrothed or married) were allowed to watch the races. Also priestesses in the temple of Zeus who lit the oil lamps were permitted.

Barbarians were allowed to watch, but not to compete. A competitor or participant had to be a free, unpunished Greek who had been trained for the games in his home for ten months, and for one month in Olympia. The prize for winning

Male participants

Participants and spectators of ancient Olympics

Women participants

an event was an olive wreath from Zeus' holy tree. The winner was allowed to raise a victory statue of Zeus. In his hometown, a winner would usually get free meals for the rest of his life! This is because they brought fame to the cities to which they belonged and the townsfolk, as well as the aristocrats glorified them.

Slaves and women, especially married ones, were strictly forbidden to watch the games. And if a woman was caught as a spectator, she was immediately thrown off Mt. Typaeon! Women could compete though in the *Heraia* games. The Heraea Games, the first recorded competition for women in the Olympic Stadium, were held in the 6th century BC. It originally consisted of foot races only, as did the competition for males. It is worth noting that like ancient Olympics even in the early years of the modern Olympics, women were not at all well represented.

In general, young girls in Ancient Greece weren't encouraged to be athletes except the Spartan girls. The Spartans believed that athletic women could breed strong warriors. So they trained girls alongside boys in sports.

After the 2012 Olympic Games are over, the new Olympic park constructed in London will become one of the largest urban parks built in Europe than since the last 150 years.

13

Closure of ancient Olympics

Theodosius I

Romans neither trained for nor participated in Greek athletics. The Olympic Games were finally abolished about AD 400 by the Roman Emperor Theodosius I or his son. The last traditional Olympiad was probably held in 393 AD. The Temple of Zeus was burnt in a fire in 426 AD. Some believe that it was demolished by a decree of Theodosius II. In the years that followed, earthquakes and floods erased all signs of the site of the ancient Olympic games forever.

The Grecian Empire was taken over by the Romans in the middle of the 2nd century BC, and the support for the competitions at Olympia and elsewhere came down considerably during the next century. The Romans looked on athletics with contempt; to strip naked and compete in public was degrading to them. Nevertheless, the Romans realized the political value of the Greek festivals. The Roman Emperor Augustus organised games for Greek athletes in a temporary wooden stadium erected near the Circus Maximus in Rome and also begun major new athletic festivals in Italy and in Greece. Emperor Nero was also a keen patron of the festivals in Greece.

Augustus Caesar

Revival of the Olympic Games

The credit of reviving the Olympics in the modern era goes to one called Pierre, Baron de Coubertin. He was born in Paris on New Year's Day, 1863. Coubertin travelled to England in 1890 to meet Dr. William Penny Brookes, who had tried for decades to revive the ancient Olympic Games, getting the idea from a series of modern Greek Olympiads held in Athens starting in 1859.

When Coubertin discussed with Brookes about physical education, Brookes was more interested in reviving the Olympic Games. He also showed him documents relating to both the Greek and the British Olympiads. On November 25, 1892, at a meeting of the Union des Sports Athlétiques in Paris, with no mention of Brookes, Coubertin himself advocated the idea of reviving the Olympic Games. It was not considered at that time. So, he placed his proposal once again in June 1894 at a conference on international sport attended by 79 delegates from 9 countries.

A great deal of indifference and part oppositions had cropped up and finally it was decided that the first modern Olympics would be held in Athens in April 1896. The Games were opened by the King of Greece in the first week of April on Greek Independence Day!

Pierre, Baron de Coubertin

Special Olympics

Special Olympics is the world's largest sports program for children and adults with *intellectual disabilities*. It provides training and competitions to more than 3.7 million athletes in more than 170 countries the whole year round. Since 1969, Special Olympics Connecticut (SOCT) has provided year-round sports training and athletic competition throughout the state through local, regional and state programs. Alternating between summer and winter, the Special Olympics World Games are held every two years.

The spirit of Olympics

The Olympic flag

The flag of the Olympic Games

The Olympic flag was created by Pierre de Coubertin in 1914. It contains five interconnected rings on a white background. The five rings symbolize the five continents. They are interconnected which symbolizes the friendship that will be gained from these international competitions. The rings, from left to right, are blue, yellow, black, green, and red. The colours were chosen because at least one of them appeared on the flag of every country in the world. The Olympic flag was first brought into use in the 1920 Olympic Games in Antwerp, Belgium. It is paraded during the opening ceremony of each Olympic Games. At the end of an Olympics, the Mayor of the host-city presents the flag to the Mayor of the next host-city. The flag remains in the town hall of the next host-city until the next Olympic Games, four years later.

Olympic flame

The tradition of the Olympic flame began during the ancient Olympic Games, over 2700 years ago in Greece. During the Ancient Olympic Games, a sacred flame was lit from the sun's rays at Olympia, and it stayed lit until the Games were over. This flame symbolised the 'endeavour for protection and struggle for victory'. It was first introduced into our Modern Olympics at Amsterdam Games in 1928. Since then, the flame symbolizes 'the light of spirit, knowledge, and life'.

Olympic torch

The Torch Relay that had begun in the Ancient Olympics was revived at the 1936 Berlin Games. For each Olympics, a new flame was lit in the ancient Olympic stadium in Olympia, Elis, Greece. The flame was lit using a parabolic mirror to focus the rays of the Sun. This flame began its Olympic Torch Relay by touring Greece.

The spirit of Olympics

Olympic torch

In the modern times, this flame is taken to the country where the games will be held. After that, the flame is then carried around this country using a series of torches carried by people who run, walk, ride horses and use other modes of transport. The last runner lights the large Olympic torch which burns throughout the games. The flame is extinguished during the closing ceremony.

The Olympic motto

The Olympic motto can be enumerated as, *Citius, Altius, Fortius*, which means Swifter, Higher, Stronger.

Olympic medals

In the Ancient Olympics, a wreath of olive branches was placed on the winner's head as olive branches were considered to be sacred.

At the modern day Olympics, each first-place winner receives a gold medal, each second-place winner receives a silver medal, and each third-place winner receives a bronze medal. Medals differ in design for each new Olympics. Certificates called *victory diplomas* are also given to many top winners in each sport.

Olive wreath

Medals

17

Olympic oath

Just as ancient Greek athletes had to swear an oath to play fairly, so do the participants in the modern Olympic Games have to do. The oath was written by Baron de Coubertin and it is taken at the Opening Ceremony by an athlete from the host country on behalf of all athletes. The Olympic oath was first taken during the 1920 Olympic Games by a Belgian fencer, Victor Boin.

Victor Boin

Astonishing fact

The oldest ever Olympian was Oscar Swahn. He was a Swedish shooter in the 1920 Antwerp, Belgium, Olympics. He was 72 years old.

The 1912 Olympics was the last time when gold medals were made of solid gold. But later, they've been silver medals with gold plating.

The Olympic creed

The Olympic creed is a doctrine or a statement of belief.

Pierre de Coubertin the reviver of modern Olympic Games got the idea for this phrase from a speech given by Bishop Ethelbert Talbot at a service for Olympic champions during the 1908 Olympic Games. The Olympic Creed reads: '*The most important thing in the Olympic Games is not to win but to take part, just as the most important thing in life is not the triumph but the struggle. The essential thing is not to have conquered but to have fought well.*'

The spirit of Olympics

The Olympic mascot

The Olympic mascots are characters usually an animal seldom a human figure native to the area where the Olympic Games are taking place. They generally represent the cultural heritage of the place.

Since the 1968 Winter Olympics in Grenoble, France the Olympic Games have began having mascots. The first major mascot in the Olympic Games was Misha in the 1980 Summer Olympics in Moscow.

> Around 3500 babies in China have been given the name Aoyun, or 'Olympics'. Countless Chinese mothers tried to give birth on the day of the opening ceremony, August 8, 2008.

The First Marathon

In 490 BCE, Pheidippides, a Greek soldier, ran from the battle grounds of Marathon to Athens (about 25 miles) to inform the Athenians that they had won. The distance was filled with hills and other obstacles. So Pheidippides arrived in Athens extremely tired and with bleeding feet. After telling the townspeople of the Greeks' victory in the battle, Pheidippides fell to the ground dead. In 1896, at the first modern Olympic Games, a race was held of approximately the same length to commemorate

Misha
1980 Summer Olympics,
Moscow, Russia

Hodori
1988 Summer Olympics,
Seoul, Korea

OLYMPICS

Pheidippides. This came to be known as a marathon after the place in Greece.

> The total cost of Beijing Olympics was around 43 billion USD! The cost of building venues amounted to around 1.8 billion USD.

ancient marathon

Modern marathon

Opening and closing ceremonies

Every Olympics has a grand opening and a closing ceremony which is organized by the host country. Like the Olympics itself, the opening and the closing ceremonies are much awaited events which generally reflect the host country's culture and heritage and of course the spirit of Olympics.

Opening ceremony olympics

20

The spirit of Olympics

Paraolympics

Paralympic Games is a major international multi-sport event where athletes who are physically disabled, compete. The term 'Paralympic' is derived from the Greek preposition meaning 'beside' or 'alongside'.

This includes athletes with amputations, mobility disabilities, cerebral palsy and blindness. Similar to the Olympics, there are Winter and Summer Paralympic Games which are held immediately after their respective Olympic Games. All Paralympic Games are governed by the International Paralympic Committee (IPC) comprising of elected representatives from around the world.

Paralympians strive to get equal treatment from non-disabled Olympic athletes, but the gap in funding between Olympic and Paralympic athletes is very large.

Paralympics

The disabilities under which athletes are allowed to participate in Paralympics are divided into six broad categories. They are *amputee, cerebral palsy, intellectual disability, wheelchair, visually impaired, and others.*

21

Paralympics 2012

The 2012 Summer Paralympic Games will take place between August 29 and September 9, 2012. The Games will be held in London, United Kingdom.

Although 2012 will be London's third Olympic Games, it will be the first Paralympic Games to be staged there. This is because Paralympics was created after the last time the city hosted in 1948.

Famous Paralympic athletes

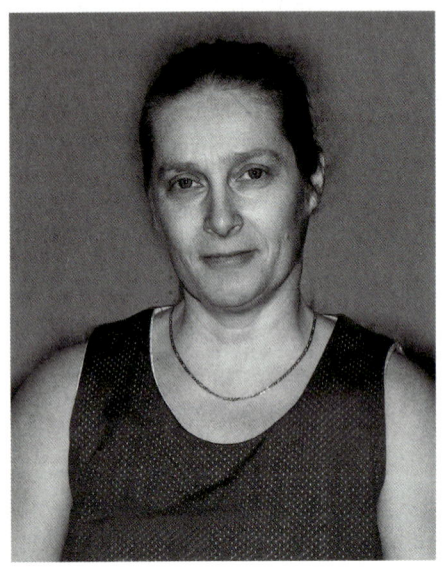

Chantal Benoit

Country : Canada

Medals won : 3 gold, 1 bronze

Chantal Benoit is one of the leading women's Wheelchair Basketball players of all time. She has competed in a total of five Paralympic Games.

In 2000 Benoit received the International Wheelchair Basketball Federation's highest honour, the Gold Medal Triad Award, for her outstanding contribution to the growth of wheelchair basketball. She was also voted Wheelchair Basketball Canada Female Athlete of the Year in the year 2008.

Bryan Kirkland

Country: USA

Medals won : 2 gold, 1 bronze

Bryan Kirkland's three Paralympic medals clearly say that he is one of the most successful Wheelchair Basketball players of the Games.

Kirkland's American team secured the first official gold when Wheelchair Rugby was included in the Games programme for the first time at Sydney 2000.

There are five types of Olympics. They are:
- Summer Olympics
- Winter Olympics
- Paralympics
- Youth Olympics
- Special Olympics

London Olympics, 2012

The 2012 Summer Olympic Games will take place in London from July 27 to August 12, 2012. London was selected as the host city on July 6, 2005 during the 117th Session of International Olympic Committee (IOC) in Singapore, defeating Moscow, New York City, Madrid and Paris. This will make London the first city to officially host the modern Olympic Games three times! London has hosted the modern Olympics in 1908 and in 1948 too. The main focus of the games this time will be a new 200 hectare Olympic Park at Stratford in the east of London. The Games will also make use of many venues which were already in place before the bid.

Olympics, 2012 at a glance

Host city : London

Country : England, United Kingdom

Dates : July 27 to August 12, 2012

Type of Olympics : Summer

Number of countries participating : 203

Mascot: Wenlock and Mandeville

Tower Bridge London

OLYMPICS

Participating countries

This time London Olympics 2012 will have 203 countries participating. The list of their names is given below in alphabetical order.

Afghanistan	Albania	Algeria	American Samoa	American Virgin Islands	Andorra	Angola	Antigua and Barbuda
Argentina	Armenia	Aruba	Australia	Austria	Azerbaijan	Bahamas	Bahrain
Bangladesh	Barbados	Belarus	Belgium	Belize	Benin	Bermuda	Bhutan
Bolivia	Bosnia and Herzegovina	Botswana	Brazil	British Virgin Islands	Brunei Darussalam	Bulgaria	Burkina Faso
Burundi	Cambodia	Cameroon	Canada	Cape Verde	Cayman Islands	Central African Republic	Chad
Chile	China	Chinese Taipei	Colombia	Comoros	Congo	Cook Islands	Costa Rica
Croatia	Cuba	Cyprus	Czech Republic	Côte d'Ivoire	Denmark	Djibouti	Dominica
Dominican Republic	DR Congo	Ecuador	Egypt	El Salvador	Equatorial Guinea	Eritrea	Estonia
Ethiopia	Fiji	Finland	France	FYR Macedonia	Gabon	Gambia	Georgia
Germany	Ghana	Great Britain & N. Ireland	Greece	Grenada	Guam	Guatemala	Guinea
Guinea-Bissau	Guyana	Haiti	Honduras	Hong Kong	Hungary	Iceland	India
Indonesia	Iran	Iraq	Ireland	Israel	Italy	Jamaica	Japan

24

Events

A list of events is given below to aid the reader who is looking for information on the events that will take place in the forthcoming Olympics.

 Archery
 Athletics
 Badminton
 Basketball
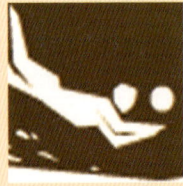 Beach Volleyball
 Boxing

 Canoe Slalom
 Canoe Sprint
 Cycling - BMX
 Cycling - Mountain Bike
 Cycling - Road
 Cycling - Track

 Diving
 Equestrian
 Fencing
 Football
 Gymnastics - Artistic
 Gymnastics - Rhythmic

 Handball
 Hockey
 Judo
 Modern Pentathlon
 Rowing
 Sailing

 Shooting
 Swimming
 Synchronised Swimming
 Table Tennis
 Taekwondo
 Tennis

 Trampoline
 Triathlon
 Volleyball
 Water Polo
 Weightlifting
 Wrestling

Olympic venues

A list of events is given below to aid the reader who is looking for information on the events that will take place in the forthcoming Olympics.

VENUE	EVENT
Aquatics Centre - Olympic Park	Diving Swimming Synchronized Swimming Modern Pentathlon
Basketball Arena - Olympic Park	Basketball Handball
BMX Track - Olympic Park	Cycling BMX
Box Hill - Out-of-London venues	Cycling Road
City of Coventry Stadium - Out-of-London venues	Football
Copper Box - Olympic Park	Modern Pentathlon Handball
Cycling - Road Race - Road events	Cycling Road
Cycling – Time Trial - Road events	Cycling Road
Earls Court - London venues	Volleyball
Energy centre - Non-competition venues	
Eton Dorney - Out-of-London venues	Rowing Canoe Sprint
ExceL - London venues	Boxing Fencing Judo Table Tennis Taekwondo Weightlifting Wrestling
Greenwich Park - London venues	Equestrian Modern Pentathlon
Hadleigh Farm - Out-of-London venues	Cycling Mountain Bike
Hampden Park - Out-of-London venues	Football
Hampton Court Palace - London venues	Cycling Road
Horse Guards Parade - London venues	Beach Volleyball
Hyde Park - London venues	Triathlon Swimming
IBC/MPC complex - Non-competition venues	

VENUE	EVENT
Lee Valley White Water Centre - Out-of-London venues	Canoe Slalom
Lord's Cricket Ground - London venues	Archery
Marathon - Road events	Athletics
Millennium Stadium - Out-of-London venues	Football
North Greenwich Arena - London venues	Gymnastics Artistic Trampoline Basketball
Old Trafford - Out-of-London venues	Football
Olympic Stadium - Olympic Park	Athletics
Olympic Village - Non-competition venues	—
Primary Substation - Non-competition venues	—
Pumping Station - Non-competition venues	
Race Walk - Road events	Athletics
Riverbank Arena - Olympic Park	Hockey
St. James' Park - Out-of-London venues	Football
The Mall - London venues	Athletics Cycling Road
The Royal Artillery Barracks - London venues	Shooting
Triathlon - Road events	Triathlon
Velodrome - Olympic Park	Cycling Track
Water Polo Arena - Olympic Park	Water Polo
Wembley Arena - London venues	Badminton Gymnastics Rhythmic
Wembley Stadium - London venues	Football
Weymouth & Portland - Out-of-London venues	Sailing
Wimbledon - London venues	Tennis

27

Olympics Hall of Fame

Female Olympians

Over the years countless sportsmen and sportswomen have participated in the Olympics. They all have a tale to tell about their experiences about their winning and losing. But only a few are remembered because of their achievements. Here are a few whose achievements are considered to be outstanding and commendable.

Mia Hamm

Country : USA

Medals won : 2 gold, 1 silver

Mia Hamm has been the most dominant women's football player of the 1990s. Hamm helped her team to win the gold medal, defeating China in the finals at the inaugural women's Olympic Football tournament in 1996.

Although the USA was beaten by Norway in the final at Sydney 2000 Olympics, four years later Hamm and the team won the gold medal, defeating Brazil 2-1 after extra time.

Teresa Edwards

Country : USA

Medals won : 4 gold, 1 bronze

The most decorated Olympic Basketball player ever, Teresa Edwards holds 2 records— as both the youngest and the oldest Olympic gold medallist in women's Basketball.

Having participated in five Games, she won a medal at each one of them. Her journey began at Los Angeles 1984 where, aged just 20, she was part of the winning USA team.

Seoul Olympics in 1988 saw Edwards at the heart of another USA triumph and, despite having to settle for a bronze at Barcelona 1992, she won gold again at both Atlanta 1996 and Sydney 2000.

Olympics Hall of Fame

Sun Hee Lee

Country : Republic of Korea

Medals won : 1 gold

Sun Hee Lee created history at Sydney 2000 by becoming the first Olympic Taekwondo champion.

She had to beat the reigning world champion just to qualify for her nation's team. But Sun stormed herself to victory at the Games, taking the 67kg title after defeating Norway's Trude Gundersen in the final. Her success can be enumerated in her own words—

'It's not the strongest who wins in taekwondo; it's the one who beats the strongest.'

Steve Redgrave

Country : Great Britain

Medals won : 5 gold, 1 bronze

Steve Redgrave is often considered to be Britain's greatest ever Olympian. He was the first athlete to win gold medals at five successive Olympic Games in an endurance sport.

At the age of 38, Redgrave competed in the Sydney 2000 Games and earned an incredible fifth gold medal!

OLYMPICS

Darrell Pace

Country : USA

Medals won : 2 gold, 1 silver

Darrell Pace, a four-time Olympian broke five Olympic records at the 1976 and 1984 Games and won two individual titles.

He first won gold at the Montreal 1976 Games, and eight years later he repeated this success in Los Angeles. Along with his Olympic success, Pace also set multiple world records in the sport and won many world and national championships.

> **Special Olympics serve more than 3.1 million athletes in 175 countries!**
>
> **Special Olympics athletes compete in more than 30,000 events every year.**

Andrey Lavrov

Country : Russia

Medals won: 3 gold, 1 bronze

Goalkeeper Andrey Lavrov was the first three-time Olympic Handball champion. He is the only athlete to have won Olympic gold medals for three different national teams!

Andrey Lavrov first competed at Seoul Games in 1988, winning a gold medal as part of the Soviet Union team. He then repeated this feat with the Unified Team four years later in Barcelona. Lavrov captained Russia to the gold medal at the Sydney 2000 Games. At the age of 42, he again became a part of the Russian Olympic team, picking up a bronze medal at Athens 2004.

Test Your MEMORY

1. Where did the Olympic Games start?
2. Initially how long was the duration of the ancient Olympic Games?
3. When did the modern Olympic Games begin? Name the man who proposed it.
4. Name at least 4 things related to Olympics from which one can feel the spirit of it.
5. Name the different kinds of Olympic Games that take place.
6. Why did the ancient Olympic Games close down? Who was responsible for it?
7. What was the reward given to the winners in the ancient times?
8. How do they differ from the rewards of the modern Olympics?
9. Name the Greek Gods & Goddesses whose temples were located in Olympia.
10. Define pancratium.
11. What do you understand by pentathlon.
12. Write about any one Olympian who is remembered in history for his achievement.

Index

A
achievements 11, 28
Altis 6, 9, 10
athletes 3, 8, 9, 10, 11, 12, 13, 14, 15, 18, 21, 22, 30

B
Barcelona 28, 30

D
dolichos 10

E
Elis 3, 6, 7, 16

G
gymnasiums 3, 6

H
Hellanodikai 10
Heraeum 6
Heraia 13
hippodrome 9, 10
hoplitodromos 11

I
International Olympic Committee 7, 23
International Paralympic Committee 21

M
Marathon 10, 19, 20, 27
mascots 19, 23

O
Olympia 3, 5, 6, 7, 8, 9, 12, 14, 16

P
pagration 11
palaestra 3, 6
pancratium 4
parabolic mirror 16
Paralympic Games 21, 22
Peloponesse 6
pentathlon 4, 10
Pheidippides 19, 20, 26, 27
Phidias 6, 8

S
Sparta 7
stadion 3, 9

T
Theodosius I 14

V
vouleutirion 9

Z
Zeus 3, 5, 6, 8, 9, 10, 11, 12, 13, 14